Simon Peter asked Him, "Lord, where
are You going?"
Jesus replied, "Where I am going,
you cannot follow now, but you will
follow later."
John 13:36 NIV

To Erik

PETER
The Fisher of Men
Retold by Anne de Graaf
Illustrated by José Pérez Montero
© Copyright 1990 by Scandinavia Publishing House
Nørregade 32, DK-1165 Copenhagen K

English-language edition published through
special arrangement with Scandinavia by
Wm. B. Eerdmans Publishing Co.,
255 Jefferson Ave. S.E., Grand Rapids, Michigan 49503
All rights reserved
Printed in Hong Kong

ISBN 0-8028-5033-2

PETER
The Fisher of Men

Written by Anne de Graaf
Illustrated by José Pérez Montero

Eerdmans

There once was a man who knew how to walk on water. There really were two men. One knew and the other tried to know. The one who knew was Jesus. The one who tried to know was called Simon Peter. He was a fisherman.

It happened one night after Simon and some of Jesus' other friends set off in a boat. Jesus didn't go with them. He wanted to climb a nearby mountain and pray.

"Cross the lake," Jesus told His men. "I'll meet up with you later." Simon and several of the others had often gone night fishing. It was the best time for catching fish. The lake was called the Sea of Galilee. They knew the hills around the lake often trapped winds. At night these winds brought storms.

"I feel the wind changing again," Simon said to his brother Andrew. The two men watched the sun sizzle into the water to the east. The lake seemed calm, but the two

fishermen knew better.

Before long, a storm hit. The wind whipped the waves around the tiny boat! The men strained at the oars. It did no good. The boat went where the storm took it.

"What should we do?" Simon shouted at John. They were the leaders of the group. But John just shook his head.

In the darkest part of the night, the storm went wild. Then suddenly, one of the men yelled. "I see a ghost! Look, there's something walking on water!"

But of course, there's no such thing as ghosts. The person they saw passing by the boat was Jesus.

"No, how can it be?" the men said to each other. They were very afraid. The wind howled in their ears. The sea spray splashed their eyes. They held on to the boat for dear life.

Jesus called out, "Don't be afraid! It's just Me, Jesus!" The wind roared. The waves formed walls around the boat. One of the little group of scared men stood up.

It was Simon. "Why, it is Jesus!" he said to the others. He stepped toward the side of the boat and took a closer look.

Jesus' feet barely touched the water. But He did not sink. The waves seemed not to touch Jesus. Wind blew His hair. But Jesus stood tall and strong.

Simon called out, "Lord, if it is You, tell me to come to You on the water."

Jesus said, "Come!"

Simon put one foot over the side. It went down, down, down, then stopped. Then he swung his second leg over and stood up. He did not sink!

Simon felt his back grow warm. He took a step. Then another and another. He watched Jesus the whole time. Simon was walking on water!

But after a few steps, he heard the wind howling. He felt the cold spray on his face. And he looked down. Then Simon forgot to trust Jesus and be brave. Instead of looking at Jesus, he looked at the waves. "How can I, just an ordinary fisherman, walk on water?" he wondered. That's when Simon began to sink. "Help! Lord, save me!" he screamed.

Right away, Jesus reached out and grabbed him. Jesus said, "Oh Simon, Simon! I told you not to be afraid! Why did you stop trying?"

Jesus and Simon climbed back into the boat. The storm stopped. The sea grew calm. Simon shook his head. Had it all been a dream? He looked up at Jesus, then out at the still sea.

As Simon watched the water, he thought about the very first time Jesus told him not to be afraid. He had looked over calm waves then, too.

On that first morning, just after sunrise, Simon had been watching the lake. Early morning mist rose off the water. "Something is different today," he said to himself. But he didn't know what.

The sea gulls caw-cawed. The rosy sun spread its light. Simon sighed. He helped his brother Andrew haul the boat up onto the beach. All night long they had fished, working together with the two sons of Zebedee, James and John. The men had worked hard, but caught nothing. When Andrew said he was going for a walk, Simon said nothing. Thinking hard about his funny feeling, Simon just picked up one of the torn nets. He started mending it.

Hours passed, and Andrew still didn't come back to help his brother. Finally, Simon heard a group of people coming his way. He looked up and saw Andrew break from the crowd and run toward him. "Here He comes, Simon! You must stop and listen to Him."

"You mean He's the one who keeps you from helping me mend the nets?" Simon growled. He waved the wooden needle at his brother. A torn net hung over his other arm.

As Andrew turned to join the crowd again, Simon called him back. "You!" the big fisherman roared. "Come help me wash this net."

Andrew did as his brother told him. But he didn't want to. Andrew kept looking over at the crowd which was heading their way.

For the rest of the morning Simon and Andrew threw the nets in and out of the water, rinsing them clean. As Simon bent over one net, picking out pieces of seaweed, he saw a shadow on the sand. He looked up. Simon saw a man standing by him.

"That's Him," he heard Andrew whisper.

"Your boat," the man said. At the sound of His voice, Simon shivered. "May I please use your boat?"

Simon nodded. He and Andrew helped the man into the boat, then pushed it into the water. Simon had no choice but to wait, as the man went on teaching the crowd on the beach.

When He had finished, the man turned to Simon. "Push the boat out into deeper water. Then let down your nets."

"But we've fished hard all night and caught nothing." Then Simon looked into the man's dark eyes again. He changed his mind. "But because You say so, I'll do it."

Simon and Andrew threw the nets overboard. Suddenly, the boat sagged. "Whoa! Look at this!" The two fishermen couldn't believe their eyes. The nets were about to break, they were so full of fish.

"Over here! Over here!" They called their partners, James and John, to bring the other boat.

"I don't believe it!"

The men sweated and strained to heave all the fish into the two boats. Even so, both boats were so full, they began to sink! That's when Simon stumbled over to Jesus.

He fell to his knees and said, "You don't even know me! Don't do this for me, I'm nobody special. Why, I'm no good at all!" Simon waved his hand at the huge catch. Fish slapped the sides of both boats. Some even wiggled their way back into the water. The men stood with their mouths open. They had never seen a catch like this.

That's when Jesus said to Simon for the first time, "Don't be afraid. Come, follow Me and I'll make you fishers of men." These were the most important words in Simon's life. He would hear them again and again and still never forget.

Simon looked back over the sea. The mist had lifted. A tingly feeling ran up his back. Now he knew why the day would be different.

As soon as the boats were beached, Simon left everything behind. He even left the catch in the boats, and that's not an easy thing for a fisherman to do. Then he followed Jesus. After that day when Simon first met Jesus, everything changed. Simon wanted something more than just to catch fish. He and Andrew, together with their partners James and John, became Jesus' best friends. They followed Him from village to village, listening and learning.

It wasn't easy. They had left everything behind. They weren't even sure who Jesus was. All Simon knew was he had to hear more.

The crowds grew larger every time Jesus taught. The people watched Jesus make sick people better, over and over again. Simon could not believe his eyes. He did know, though, that every time Jesus looked at him, Simon wanted to please Him. Still, when all these people asked him who Jesus was, Simon wasn't so sure.

11

One day Jesus asked the men around Him, "Tell Me, who do the people say I am?"

His followers sat in a circle. "Some say John the Baptist. Others say Elijah. Some say You're one of the great men from the past, come back to life."

Jesus said, "But what about you? Who do you say I am?"

The dark eyes rested on Simon. He felt pushed from inside to say, "You're the Messiah, the Son of the living God." He held his breath.

Jesus said, "Ah, Simon, the only way you could know this is if My Father in heaven told you. You're blessed by God in a special way. Now listen, your name is Simon, but from now on you shall be called Peter." That meant "Rock."

"I'm calling you Peter because someday you'll lead the people who follow Me. They are My Church. You'll become the rock on which the Church is built. That means when you're their leader, it will be your job to teach people what is right and wrong. You'll be the most important person in building up the group who will follow Me."

Peter's eyes grew round. The others looked at him strangely. "Is this what it means to be a 'fisher of men'?" he asked himself. Now Peter knew one thing for sure. The next time someone asked who Jesus was, he wouldn't shake his head. He knew Jesus came straight from heaven. He was God's very own Son!

13

Peter followed Jesus all over the country, watching and learning. The weeks became months. For over two years Peter listened to Jesus. The more he learned the more he wanted to know.

Strange and wonderful things happened during those years. Peter watched Jesus help blind people to see and the crippled to walk.

One day Peter even saw the two great men Moses and Elijah visit Jesus from heaven. They stood and talked with Jesus on a mountaintop, all white and shining!

Afterward Jesus said, "Don't tell anyone what you've seen today until I've risen from the dead."

Peter and his friends didn't know what Jesus meant. " 'Risen from the dead'? Is Jesus going to die?" they asked. It didn't take long

for them to find out.

Not everyone liked Jesus. He had enemies. Most of the religious leaders hated Jesus. They wanted to kill Him. There were also so many people who loved Jesus, though, that Peter and his friends thought Jesus was safe. They were wrong.

It happened one night in Jerusalem. Jesus and His friends had eaten dinner together. All evening long Jesus had talked about how He would soon be killed, but then come back to life again. "Tonight, none of you will help Me," Jesus said.

Peter didn't like that kind of talk. He stood

up and said angrily, "What do You mean? The others might leave You, but I'll always stand by You!"

Jesus shook His head. "Ah, Peter. Don't you know? Tonight, before the rooster crows, you'll say you never knew Me. You'll do this three times."

"No! No, I'd die for You. I'll never, ever lie about knowing You!" The other men said the same. Jesus said nothing.

After dinner, Jesus and His men climbed a hill to a special garden. Jesus wanted to pray to God. He was very sad. His heart felt as though it would break and He had a huge lump in His throat. He didn't want to die. He asked Peter, James and John, "Stay with Me and pray."

Jesus prayed as hard as He could. He was so torn up inside about what He had to do, Jesus sweat tears of blood. But where was Peter? Where was the "Rock"? He had fallen asleep!

15

16

"Peter! Couldn't you even stay awake to help Me pray? A terrible night is ahead of us. Try and help Me!"

Peter tried and tried. More than anything, he wanted to help Jesus. The night was warm, though. No matter how hard he tried

not to, something made Peter close his eyes as he leaned up against a tree. The next thing he knew, Jesus was shaking him awake for a third time.

"Are you still asleep? Look, it's too late! Here come My enemies to take Me away!"

Peter looked where Jesus pointed. Soldiers! A mob of angry people headed their way. They carried torches and swords! Peter jumped up. Fear turned his stomach over. He grabbed Andrew. "They wouldn't dare take Jesus!" Both men knew Jesus had many friends, but He also had many enemies.

"Where can we run?" Peter looked around the moonlit garden. There was nowhere to go. They were trapped!

One of the men who had been a follower of Jesus walked with the soldiers and priests. He had told Jesus' enemies, "The one I go up to is the one you should take prisoner."

This man's name was Judas. Peter watched Judas hug Jesus and kiss Him on the cheek. He said, "Teacher!"

"Do what you have to," Jesus said quietly.

Then the soldiers moved in. They grabbed Jesus and started taking Him away. "This is a nightmare!" Peter gasped. Jesus' enemies acted angry and mean. "You can't take the Teacher away!" Peter bellowed.

Peter shook himself, quickly looked around and grabbed his short sword. Then he ran toward the crowd. Waving the sword, Peter yelled, "Leave the Teacher alone!"

With a mighty "Swish!" the sword cut off a slave's ear! Peter stared at the ear. Then he remembered Jesus' talk about death. The bad dream was coming true!

"Stop it!" Jesus cried. "Put your sword back. Don't you know that anyone who uses the sword, usually will die by the sword?" Then Jesus touched the slave's ear and made him better!

He turned to Peter, "If I wanted to, I could ask My Father to send thousands of angels to fight for Me. But no, I'm going to do My Father's mission. If you fight them, I can't do what I came here to do. Peter," He looked into the fisherman's eyes, "don't be afraid."

Just as Jesus finished speaking, the guards dragged Him away. By then all the other disciples had fled. Peter felt torn. Should he run and hide as the others had, or should he try and help Jesus somehow? "I can't follow! They might come and take me away too!" So Peter ran and hid behind an olive tree. Despite Jesus' words, the big man trembled with fear.

Peter waited until the soldiers had marched down to the bottom of the hill. Then he followed, hiding behind trees and houses as he went. The priests and soldiers brought Jesus to a courtyard.

There the guards built a fire to keep themselves warm. The priests and other religious leaders began to question Jesus. Peter didn't know what to do. "What will happen to Jesus?" he grumbled to himself. He took a deep breath and crept into the courtyard. Peter sat down by the fire with the guards. It would be a long night.

He hoped no one would notice him. But a servant girl stared at Peter for a few moments. She said, "You were with Jesus of Nazareth."

Peter looked over his shoulders. "I hope no one heard her!" he thought. "If the guards find out who I am, they'll kill me."

"No! No!" he said loud enough for everyone to hear. "I don't know what you're talking about!"

Peter hugged himself. He was the only one of Jesus' disciples in the courtyard. All the others had run away. "I'd better not stay by this fire," he thought.

Peter walked toward the gateway. There another girl saw him. She said, "This man was with Jesus."

Peter swore, "I don't even know Him!"

After a little while, a group of men standing nearby came up to Peter. One of the men knew the slave whose ear Peter had sliced off. "Didn't I see you in the garden with that Jesus? I'm sure of it," he said. "You're one of Jesus' friends. Why, we can hear you're both from the same place just by the way you talk!"

By now, Peter was so afraid, he swore again and again. "I don't even know the man!"

No sooner were the words out of Peter's mouth, than he heard a rooster crow. Just then, Jesus turned and looked straight at Peter. Peter's heart broke. Jesus had said, "Before the rooster crows, you'll say you don't know Me three times."

Peter hid his face in his hands. It seemed as though his very world had crumbled. He staggered out of the courtyard, weeping every step of the way.

During the dark days ahead, Peter felt himself grow old and tired. The day after Jesus was arrested, His enemies killed Him, hanging Jesus on a cross. Peter watched it happen. It burned him inside. It hurt so much, Peter felt numb.

He and some of the other men and women went into hiding. They were afraid the soldiers and priests might take them away and kill them. "If they can arrest and kill Jesus, they could do it to us," Peter told them.

They had forgotten what Jesus so often had taught them, "Don't be afraid."

A few days later, a woman who belonged to this group of Jesus' followers burst through the door of their hiding place. She ran up to Peter and his old fishing partner, John. "Something terrible has happened! They've taken Jesus' body away! He's not in the cave anymore!"

Peter looked at John. John looked at Peter. Without another word, the two dashed off to the garden where Jesus was buried in a cave. They tore down the streets. Peter had never run so fast before in his life. He panted and raced, but John still beat him. At the cave, they stopped.

John looked in. Peter shot past him and entered the cave. "Nothing!" He panted at John. "She's right. There's nothing here but the cloths Jesus was wrapped in!"

The two men bent double, trying to catch their breath. "It's no use," John said. "We'd better get back to the others."

After a few moments they left, shaking their heads. "The priests must have stolen His body!" Peter clenched his fists. "I have to find out what's going on!" Peter wouldn't have long to wait.

That evening the men and women huddled together in the attic room where they were hiding. "Do you think the soldiers will kill us, too?" they asked each other. No one knew. They had locked the doors to be on the safe side.

Suddenly, a shape passed through the wall! It was Jesus! The men gasped. The women screamed!

"Peace!" Jesus told them. And again He said, "Don't be afraid, it's Me." He showed them the sores on His hands and side.

"It really is Jesus!" The horror on Peter's face turned to joy. He and the rest were so happy they didn't know what to say. Peter felt a great weight lift off his shoulders. "Oh Teacher, Teacher," he cried. The huge fisherman fell to the floor on his knees. Tears streamed down his cheeks.

Peter saw Jesus several times after He rose from the dead. One of those times was when Peter and some of his friends wanted to get some food for the others. So they went fishing. They spent all night on the lake. By morning their boat was still empty.

"Caught anything?" A stranger called out from the beach.

"No," the fishermen answered. The stranger stood with the rising sun behind him. Peter and the others could not see that actually, he was Jesus!

The men brought the boat closer to shore.

Jesus said, "Throw your net over the right-hand side of the boat! Then you'll find some fish."

The men were so tired they didn't even argue. Within minutes the net came back full! John squinted at the stranger. "It's Him!" he shouted. "It's the Lord!" John grabbed Peter.

"You're right!" Peter said. "Only Jesus could have filled the net like this. It's the same miracle as what happened on that first day I met Him!" Peter quickly pulled on some clothes and jumped into the water. He

forgot to breathe, he swam so hard. "It's really Him, it's really Him!" He kept saying to himself.

Once on shore, Peter wouldn't leave Jesus' side. The others brought in the boat. Peter helped Jesus fry some fish for them over a fire. While they ate, John said to Peter, "This is just like old times, isn't it?" Peter nodded and grinned, his mouth full of fish.

After the meal, Jesus called Peter to one side. He wanted to talk in private. "Peter, do you really love Me? Do you love Me more than these others do?"

Peter gasped. "Of course, Lord! Why, You know I love You."

"Then take care of My sheep." Jesus was telling Peter to take care of all the people he would someday lead closer to God. Jesus asked His question three times. Each time, Peter answered yes.

Jesus finished by saying that Peter would indeed lead Jesus' followers well. He also said that Peter would die a terrible death. When Peter's eyes grew round, Jesus said, "Don't be afraid. Just follow Me."

Even though Peter had seen and heard Jesus with his own eyes and ears, he still felt afraid. He and the others were scared the priests and soldiers might take them away and kill them.

They just did not know what to do. Every time Jesus saw them, He said, "Don't be afraid." It didn't help much until Jesus added a promise. "Soon I'll send you a Helper."

On the day when the Helper arrived, Peter finally stopped being afraid.

He was upstairs praying with his friends. Suddenly a sound like the blowing of a strong wind filled the house. "Whoosh!"

"What's that?" the others asked.

Small lights like flames rested on the heads of Peter, John, Andrew and the others. It was the Helper, God's Holy Spirit, come to make Jesus' followers strong and brave!

Peter shook himself. What had happened? He didn't care anymore about being arrested! "We must tell more people about Jesus!" he told his friends. "No matter what, they must know!"

The people outside had heard the strange sound like wind. Because this was a busy city, they came from countries all over the world. In their different languages they asked, "We heard an odd sound hit your house. What happened?"

Peter spoke and no one could believe what they heard! "How can that simple fisherman

speak so many different languages?" In the ears of thousands of people it sounded as if Peter came from their very own hometowns.

"Listen!" he shouted. "Jesus, the great Teacher Jesus is really the Son of God! You had Him killed, but now God has brought Him back to life again! Don't be afraid! Believe in Him and He'll change your lives! Follow Jesus!"

Peter's message cut into the hearts of over three thousand people. They all felt sorry about living bad lives. They wanted to start over again. They asked Jesus to forgive them and help them. These were the first Christians and Peter became their first leader.

All the people who believed in Jesus prayed together. They learned from Peter and his friends. Those who were rich shared their money and things with those who were poor. No man or woman was better off than any other.

Even though there were many who believed what Peter preached, many more called him a liar. The same religious leaders who killed Jesus, wanted to kill Peter.

Thanks to the Holy Spirit, Peter wasn't afraid anymore. "The most important thing is to share Jesus with as many people as possible!" He traveled far and wide to share the Good News.

All the same, it didn't take long before Peter's enemies had him arrested. The first time this happened, Peter showed such bravery, everyone was amazed.

"He's just a fisherman, how does he know what he's talking about!"

"Such courage!"

"Ah yes, wasn't he with that Jesus?" And his enemies let Peter go free.

The second time Peter was arrested he had a harder time of it. The terrible King Herod did not like the Christians. He had already killed James, one of Peter's fishing friends. Now he wanted to kill Peter.

"Arrest him! Chain that man to a soldier so he won't get away!"

"We warned him to stop talking about that Jesus!"

"Now he'll learn his lesson!"

Poor Peter! He sat in a damp and dirty prison cell. The next day Herod would surely have him killed in order to please Peter's enemies. Chained to two soldiers as he slept, Peter didn't have much reason to hope.

Even so, Peter wasn't afraid. Peter trusted Jesus. The other Christians also trusted Jesus. They prayed and waited, hoping that somehow their leader might go free.

That night as Peter slept, a very strange thing happened! Someone shook him. He opened his eyes and saw a bright angel! "Hurry!" the angel said. "Get up and come with me!"

As the angel spoke, the chains fell off Peter's arms! "Put your cloak on and follow me," the angel said.

Peter did as the angel told him. "I must be dreaming," he thought as he walked right past the snoring guards. "No one can see me!"

Once outside, the iron gate leading to the city opened all by itself! Then the angel disappeared. Peter stood still, waiting for the sounds of shouting and running feet. "Nothing! How can that be?" he asked himself.

"God set me free and the guards didn't see a thing!" Peter ran to a friend's house. Many people were gathered there, praying for Peter.

He knocked on the door. A servant came, but she was so excited to hear Peter's voice, she ran off before opening the door!

Peter's friends told the servant, "You're crazy! There's no way Peter can be standing outside. We're praying for him right now!"

But Peter kept knocking. Finally his friends opened up for him. "Peter!" Everyone hugged him and wanted to hear his story.

The next morning the king searched for Peter, but could not find him. The guards scratched their heads. Then the evil King Herod punished his guards by putting them all to death.

In the years to come, the Christians' enemies became more and more terrible. They arrested and killed many believers. Peter led the Christians bravely. He was no longer the unsure, stubborn fisherman Jesus had first met.

Peter became a true fisher of men. Peter's words helped people all over the world to want to know more about Jesus. Peter even let others hurt him, rather than say he did not love Jesus. He led the Christians, and whenever their enemies made them suffer, Peter felt the pain, too.

When Peter died, he went to heaven. Many people think Peter died on a cross, just like Jesus. They say Peter's enemies hung him upside down. At that final moment, no doubt Jesus was right at Peter's side. Maybe Jesus even whispered the same words He had already spoken so often to His friend the fisherman. "Don't be afraid, Peter. Follow Me."

You can find the story of Peter in the New Testament Gospels of Matthew, Mark, Luke and John, as well as the Acts of the Apostles, chapters 1-15.